The Daily Telegraph

FLOOD

PART 1 OCTOBER 9-22 2000

The floods that began to ravage Britain in October were heralded by continuing rain reinforced by gale-force winds and waves that pounded the South Coast.

Terrible weather, even for October: that was the general reaction. But the mood turned darker when, soon after, the incessant rains swelled the rivers of Kent and East Sussex. They burst their banks, flooding major towns such as Lewes and Uckfield. Many smaller towns and villages were hit, farms were devastated and communities were cut off. Shops and businesses closed. The railways came to a halt, not only in the worst-affected areas but over a vast swathe of the South-East.

Yet this, as it turned out, was only the beginning. New storms swept across Britain, hard on the heels of the first, this

The flood waters rise and suddenly everyday life comes to a halt

time passing further north. Within days the rains that fell on hillsides began to course down into major rivers that could not cope. Vast areas of flood plains soon stood under water and urban centres such as York, Shrewsbury, Worcester and Gloucester were hit. Though storms and torrential rains like these affect Britain from time to time, they are infrequent enough to shock the generation that has to face them.

Britain in 2000 suffered the heaviest rainfall since 1903 and almost certainly the most widespread flooding since the notorious year of 1947. In short, we have all just lived through a truly historic passage of weather and natural catastrophe. With luck, we shall not see its like again. This commemorative book, compiled by The Daily Telegraph, records what happened.

···· The weather that ravaged Britain

A photo-report

W. F. Deedes

The Daily Telegraph **Flood** 3

Susan Harmer is airlifted from her farm
after being trapped by the rising
River Ouse at Offham, near Lewes.
Her husband, John, was also rescued

NIGEL BOWLES, CCNNOR

FLOOD

Part 1
October 9-22 2000

Part 2
October 28 - November 15

Firefighters and lifeboatmen wade through the high waters that devastated Uckfield town centre, East Sussex

From the waters surfaced hidden human qualities

W.F. Deedes
reflects on the countless acts of kindness that will never be reported and how, for some, things are never going to be the same again

A woman stranded by the floods surveys the scene in Lewes from her upstairs flat. Across the country the rising waters left a lasting mark

April may be the cruellest month, but October is more shocking. It was mid-October in 1987 when southern England, lashed by the worst storm of the century, lost thousands of trees. In the same month this year, it suffered the worst flood havoc for years.

We can observe philosophically that by comparison with, say, Bangladesh or Mozambique or even mid-America, violent Nature lays a relatively light hand on this island. None of that offers much joy to those whose homes were flooded – some of them twice or more, as the deluge carried on well into November.

So we need sharply to separate those of us who were merely inconvenienced by a phenomenal rainfall from that luckless minority who are still cleaning up their sitting rooms, carpets and furnishings. We will come back to them. As for the rest of us, the stormy days proved more of a challenge than anything else.

It was tiresome waiting for trains that failed to arrive, but there were compensations. I drew deep satisfaction from negotiating a flooded road in Kent. Ha, I said to myself, here is something I learned back in Army days – how to drive through flood without drowning the engine. My pleasure was enhanced by a feeling that most people on the road would not have been in the Army and so might well get stuck. The deepest floods don't alter our human nature.

Many of us in afflicted areas such as Kent and Sussex learned more about our topography. "I'd no idea this county had a river that could burst its banks," a stranger said to me as we boarded a train to London. (All emergencies help the English to become less tongue-tied.) It was satisfying to be able to tell him that it is the course of the river Medway that separates Maids and Men of Kent in the east from Kentish Maids and Men in the west.

By their nature, floods present obstacles to those who hunt for someone to blame after all national mishaps. But it was permissible to suggest that man's activities were changing the climate – for the worse – and that we had built too many new houses in areas liable to flood. The Met Office wisely refused to say whether or not the floods could be linked to man-made global warming; but predicted we might be in for

more extreme weather. I wonder about that. Looking back, one notes that when the Thames burst its banks in January 1928, 14 people drowned, and the Tate Gallery and the Palace of Westminster were flooded. In 1947 we had a prolonged freeze-up, not matched since then; and when the thaw came, towns such as Shrewsbury were flooded. There was Lynmouth in 1952, where a freak flood killed 36 people and left many homeless.

In 1953 the East Coast was devastated by flooding and upwards of 300 people drowned. I helped to report that event and for the first and last time in my life put the hire of a boat on my expenses. True, we have built up our coastal defences since then and the Thames has a barrage. But has our climate really changed for the worse?

Let us return to the real victims of the floods who temporarily lost their homes. I saw one or two of them at Yalding in Kent. You might suppose that after a spell of mopping up and drying out life went back to normal. Oh, no. Flood water brings the drains up. In some flooded houses the pong was defiant. The ground floors were not simply sodden, they were defiled.

And for the stricken home-owner, that was only the opening blow. There were more losses to come. When your house has been damaged by floodwater, do you claim insurance? In doing so you certify your home as being liable to flood and therefore knock quite a bit off the value. For members of our "property-owning democracy" that may represent a lot of savings. That is what the floods have cost many proud home-owners throughout our land.

So, let us salute the firemen and the police, the boatmen and the helicopter pilots who came to the rescue. These pages well illustrate the sort of hazards they faced. There were countless acts of kindness that will never be reported. Such emergencies do draw out human qualities which otherwise lie dormant.

But let us also remember those who feel that after this visitation their homes will never be quite the same again. Against Nature in her October and November mood the compensation culture is of little avail. For most of us the floods were a passing adventure. On some they have left a lasting mark.

'LAND AHOY!'

Treacherous floods that rose in the darkness

The rain began on Monday, October 9. The Environment Agency, newly entrusted with flood precautions, issued basic flood warnings – a kind of amber alert – affecting 17 rivers as far apart as the Yorkshire Ouse and the Dart in Devon. Of particular concern were the Kent and Sussex rivers and their notoriously vulnerable – and in part tidal – flood basins, while a sharp weather eye was kept on gathering gales heading for the South Coast.

Bognor Regis, on the West Sussex coast, took the first hit; people were evacuated from their homes in what was generally regarded, except by those who endured it, as minor flooding. The Environment Agency sent an emergency planning team to watch developments. They turned out to be more dramatic than anyone could have envisaged.

On Tuesday, the rain dropped neither gently nor mercifully upon the earth beneath. The police put out so many flood warning signs that they ran out. It intensified on Wednesday; people were warned not to travel. By Thursday, many couldn't even if they wanted to. Major defences were showing signs of cracking. The EA issued 16 severe flood warnings – its full-scale red alert – covering Kent and Sussex alone, including the Ouse, Teise, Eden and Medway.

In the small hours of Thursday, October 12, night workers and those living above shops in Uckfield, East Sussex, had to be rescued as the normally placid River Uck surged into the main shopping area. A jeweller almost died when he tried to check his stock, only to be trapped by rapidly rising water which seized him in a great wave and swept him a mile down river before rescuers could reach him.

Lifeboatmen from Poole, Brighton, Shoreham, Eastbourne and Hastings, more used to launching lifeboats into stormy seas, were called into action inland, in one instance saving the lives of six children who had been playing by a railway line when the flood waters engulfed them. RNLI volunteers ferried trapped families to safety across waterlogged East Sussex, where the catastrophe was initially concentrated.

One crew had to scramble to safety when their boat was pulled under a bridge in the ancient castle town of Lewes, where a newly built retaining wall collapsed, releasing the swollen, tidal Ouse into the lower streets.

The town's fire crew had to be rescued from their HQ and 19 brewery workers were winched to safety as an internal wall collapsed. In Lamberhurst, not far from Tunbridge Wells, the high street was under three feet of water when the Teise broke free, flooding 50 houses. Electricity workers were airlifted into their headquarters in Robertsbridge to deal with a power cut.

The small rural community of Etchingham, which lies at the conjunction of three rivers, the Dudwell, Limden and Rother, found its ancient heritage threatened as the waters invaded its 14th-century parish church, which contains some of the oldest and largest medieval funeral brasses in existence. All were submerged beneath the corrosive, polluted water. To make matters worse, a mile and a half of railway line was swept away.

The drama and the danger was not confined to towns. John and Susan Harmer were trying to tend to livestock on their farm near Lewes when the waters surrounded them. They were lucky to be spotted from the air and were hauled to safety by a coastguard helicopter which was, like the RNLI, on unaccustomed inland duty. The cattle were less fortunate: when Mrs Harmer returned on Friday, calves and cows had been swept away and 50 lambs had perished.

In Kent, people living in Maidstone woke on Thursday to find the Medway had invaded their homes. The unlucky hamlet of Five Oak Green found water coming through doors and windows for the third time in less than a year. The Stour escaped its bounds near Godmersham. And still the waters rose. Throughout Thursday night and Friday a massive evacuation exercise was under way in the villages of Yalding, East Peckham, Laddingford, Collier Street and Stilebridge as flood barriers at Tonbridge were opened to let rising waters escape.

In Tonbridge itself, the Army was sent in to bring 60 people to safety. The Medway finally burst its banks and a huge wave wreaked havoc as it raced through Maidstone. In Yalding, firefighters had to rescue 47 people and their pets from houses that were under seven feet of water. Eight businessmen were trapped in the village's 400-year-old tavern, stranded upstairs along with 14 staff without light and heat. They survived for three days on beer and sandwiches provided by the landlady, Ann Long.

But if the floods themselves were frightening, the aftermath, during the following week, was sickening. As the flooding had progressed, the water had become more and more polluted with rotting garbage and raw sewage.

Nowhere was the problem worse than in Uckfield – renamed Yuckfield by locals – as the waters drained away. The town's sewage works had crumpled under the pressure of the floods, filling the streets, shops and homes with a nauseating stench. Across the devastated area people returning in continuing rain to homes and businesses were warned that their premises might not be properly habitable for six months. By the end of the week-long drama, the region faced a bill of £300 million or more.

The insurance claims went in and the exhausted emergency services and volunteers allowed themselves some respite. Roads reopened and trains struggled to resume some sense of normality.

But the break in the weather was to turn out to be merely a lull; meteorological forces were regrouping to unleash themselves on enormous swathes of the whole country. On Saturday, October 28, Nature's second visitation began – and Bognor Regis was once again to be the harbinger of what lay in store…

A young resident of Uckfield is carried to safety by a fireman. Parts of the High Street had been under six feet of water at one stage

Where the floods struck The rivers rose to take their toll on

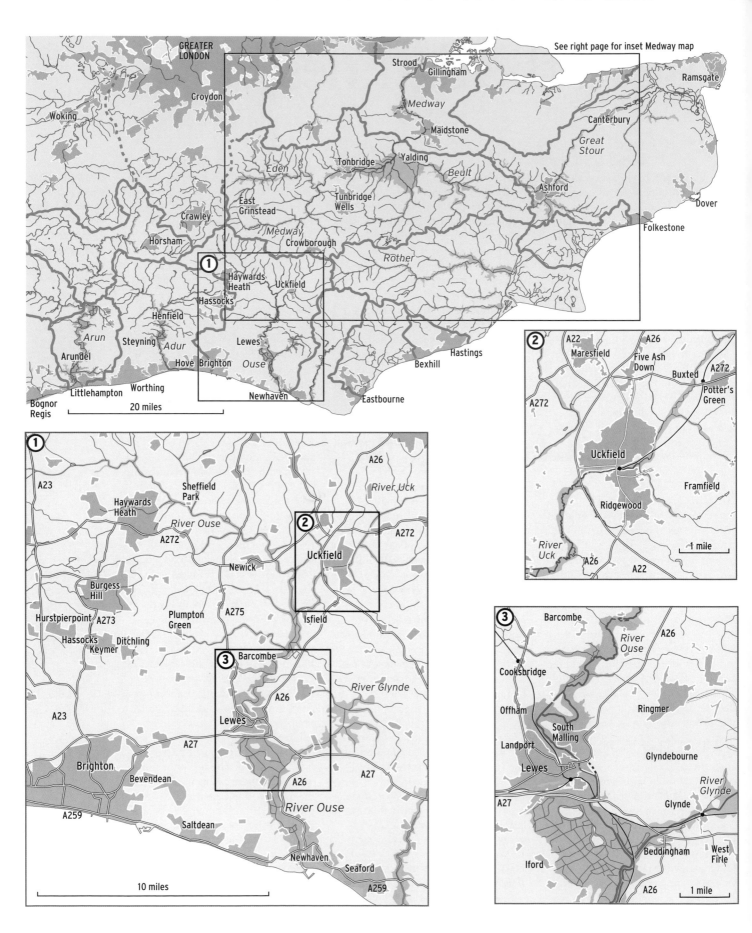

Key to flood maps

 Fluvial flood

 Mixed fluvial & coastal

 Coastal flood

 Lake river river

 River catchment area (main map, above)

 Town village railway & station

 M-way A road A dual-c

town and village life in Kent and Sussex

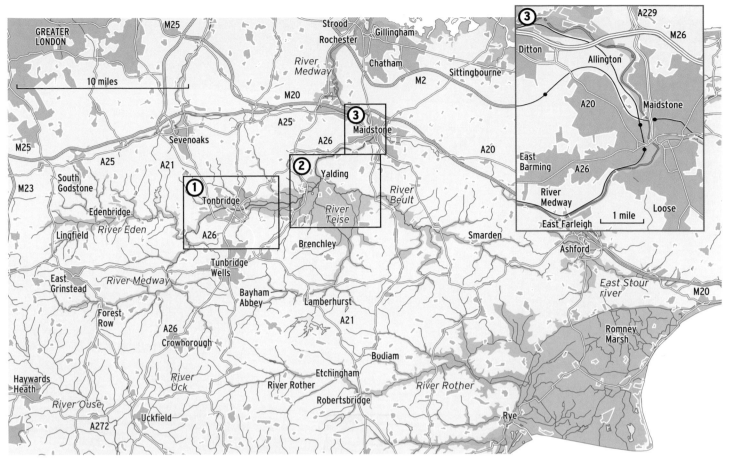

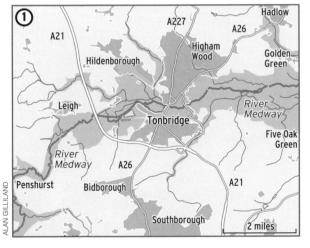

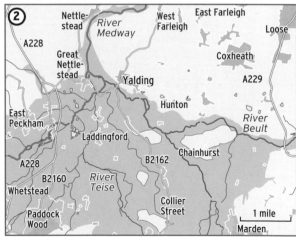

ALAN GILLILAND

Research by the Environment Agency before the deluge showed that only one person in 20 living in flood-risk areas took the threat of flooding seriously enough to prepare for damage. The agency has committed itself to ensuring that there will be minimal encroachment on flood plains by the 23 million new homes planned over the next 15 years

Warning system Forecasters worked 24 hours a day

Nearly two million properties lie on the flood plains of England and Wales, with the greatest concentration of population at risk living in the South-East. As these maps of the stricken areas of Kent and West and East Sussex confirm, the autumn 2000 floods almost exactly covered the areas proclaimed to be at risk by the Environment Agency – the Government body responsible for issuing flood warnings.

"We feel that our warning systems worked well and were very accurate," said Emer O'Connell, a spokeswoman for the Environment Agency. The agency set up a new National Flood Warning Centre earlier in the year. It promised to spend more than £100 million over the next 10 years on research to enhance its services and raise awareness and understanding of flood risk.

"Our flood forecasters work 24 hours a day, with river monitoring stations taking constant readings," Miss O'Connell explained. "When a trigger level is reached, warnings are issued." These come in stages: Flood Watch – suggesting people keep an eye open for possible inundation; Flood Warning – get ready; and Severe Flood Warning – imminent danger to life and property. Once a flood warning is issued it goes to the emergency services automatically.

The agency was formed in 1996 and was given the powers of the old National Rivers Authority. Its campaign message during Flood Action Week, just a month before Kent and East Sussex were plunged under water, was "Flooding. You can't prevent it. You can prepare for it."

Lewes

The railway station in Lewes became an icon of the Great Floods as the torrents came to a still calm. The River Ouse once brought prosperity to the town. In October 2000 it brought misery

Lewes railway station is transformed into a canal

STEVE DENNETT, CONNORS

A river patrol on the lookout for any children who may be in danger is interrupted dramatically when the lifeboat crew has to scramble to safety as strong currents drag their boat under the High Street bridge. All children in the town are accounted for, but police close the bridge and evacuate the shops

The River Ouse bursts its banks after a month's rain falls in a single day. Many residents of Lewes are rescued by the emergency services, but property and countless irreplaceable possessions are ruined

ALASTAIR GRANT, AP

A lifeboatman wades through rising water, checking whether houses need evacuation. Below, The Spinneys, where many homeowners are caught out

High tide visits Orchard Road where it is unsafe to venture outside. Below: a drowned cow's final resting place, at the front door of Lewes resident Carol Kriste

Inflatable dinghies play a vital part in rescue operations throughout Lewes. But many residents, top and above left, rely on the strong arms of the emergency services.
Left: two lifeboatmen carry Mrs Doreen Brett from her flooded home while one of their colleagues, above, takes Cha Cha, her pet dog, to safety.
Right: Malling Street, where high tides boost the water level

Above: barrels of beer float away from Harveys, Sussex's oldest independent brewery, where 19 workers have to be winched to safety by coastguard helicopter when a wall collapses.
Below left: Nicola Smith tries to salvage what she can from the ruins of her living room.
Below right: Bob Russell realises he is fighting a losing battle as he attempts to clear up the mess in his home

Above: an experience an elderly resident of Lewes is unlikely to forget as she receives some assistance from firemen to make her escape from a flooded old people's home.
Right: the owners of these vehicles face an unwelcome sight when the time comes to collect them from this car park in Lewes

The surreal reflections of homes in Thomas Street, Lewes, where overnight tides had imported pieces of debris from around the neighbourhood. The watermarks ac

the houses indicate that the tide has by now dropped around two feet from the level it had reached when at its height

Uckfield

When the floods arrived in October it was the third time in the year 2000 that the River Uck had burst its banks. Much of this country town, on the southern edge of Ashdown Forest, was under six feet of water

Lifeboatmen race to one of many rescues in the streets of Uckfield

...appy to have the road to themselves as they glide between the signs on the edge of Uckfield town centr...

With the passage of years, many roads in East Sussex have become totally inadequate for the

Water cascades violently outside a supermarket in the centre of Uckfield, leaving debris to hang untidily from the railings

Barcombe

The owners of the 14th-century Anchor Inn at Barcombe, near Lewes, describe their lovely establishment as having a "garden available, near water". This was somewhat of an understatement when the rains came down. The Anchor Inn can be seen in splendid

After six inches of rainfall in just 12 hours, the repair bill for damaged buildings and personal possessions is put initially at £100 million.
Filthy water poses a health hazard as sewers overflow, and, when the water clears, a thick layer of silt and debris remains. The fire service, top, helps residents as cars become stranded throughout Uckfield town centre.
Left: cycling routes, like all other routes, are impassable

With the passage of years, many roads in East Sussex have become totally inadequate for the ever-increasing volume of traffic, but, for today, two boys in a dinghy

Town Centre B 2102

Super-store

Bellbrook Ind. Estate

Station

appy to have the road to themselves as they glide between the signs on the edge of Uckfield town centre

The inland town of Uckfield is
unaccustomed to the presence of
lifeboatmen on duty in its streets.
But here, members of the RNLI have
to use boats and ladders as well
as their skills and strength.
The waters cut up rough at times, as
the main picture shows, and boats
have to be manhandled to keep them
on course. But despite the men's
efforts there is little that can be done
to prevent widespread damage to
cars and property

ALASTAIR GRANT, AP

JOHN COBB

SCOTT INGLETON, CASSIDY AND LEIGH

Far left: after making his way through the watery streets, a boy claims his own little island to dry off. No one is forgotten as rescue operations are mounted in Uckfield, and that includes a forlorn teddy, plucked by another youngster from the currents

Stores and eating places were left counting the cost as they became inaccessible. Below: a garden shed has made its own way to the station

A tidal wave appears as a delivery truck tries to make its way through the flooded streets. Below: two boys negotiate a garage forecourt in their dinghy

Water cascades violently outside
a supermarket in the centre
of Uckfield, leaving debris to hang
untidily from the railings

DYLAN MARTINEZ, REUTERS

DYLAN MARTINEZ, REUTERS

Clockwise from top left:
A gas inspector checks for leaks
in a supermarket.
Shopping washed out of the shops
mounts up behind street railings.
The next journey of these showroom
cars is to be to the scrapyard.
With the odds stacked against him,
a cyclist tries to pedal himself
out of trouble

CHRIS GORMAN, KENT/SUSSEX NEWS

JOHN COBB

Henfield
Close to Henfield is the headquarters of the Sussex Wildlife Trust, the starting point of a popular nature trail. It was soon to become a no-go area

JAMES BOARDMAN, KENT NEWS & PICTURES LTD

DAVID MCHUGH, SUSSEX PICTURE AGENCY

DAVID MCHUGH, SUSSEX PICTURE AGENCY

Visitors are usually attracted to the wetlands and woodlands around Henfield, which is home to a variety of wildlife. But as the River Adur's swollen waters cover the roads and fields for miles around, motorists take to their cars at their peril

Barcombe

The owners of the 14th-century Anchor Inn at Barcombe, near Lewes, describe their lovely establishment as having a "garden available, near water". This was somewhat of an understatement when the rains came down. The Anchor Inn can be seen in splendid

isolation after the River Ouse had overflowed its banks. But out of Barcombe came one piece of good news: Julia Black, 36, was rescued by tractor and then lifeboat when she went into labour. She later gave birth in a water tank to an 8lb 3oz baby boy at Crowborough Hospital

A herd of stranded cows closes
ranks to save themselves from the
flooded River Adur, near Uckfield.
Many cattle were to drown as
fields became submerged

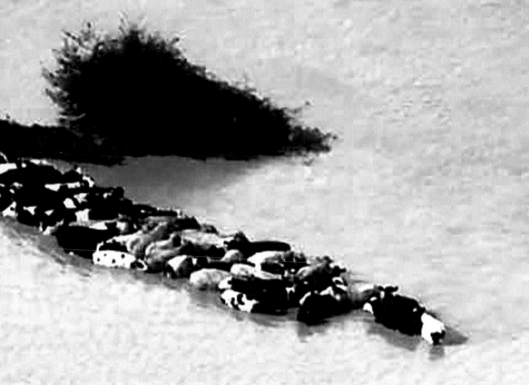

Bevendean

Some lorry drivers had to desert their cabs and swim to safety as seven inches of rain fell in the space of three days, flooding this ancient district of Brighton

Left: Alan and David Jupp are prisoners in their own home. Above: the waters keep rising. Below: Lorrie Instone and John Mack are trapped in a pub

Five Oak Green

Angry villagers reprimanded motorists for ignoring 'road closed' signs and sending even more water into their homes

Firemen carry out pumping operations in Five Oak Green, near Maidstone; would-be property sellers may now face a long wait to find buyers

Homes and caravans near the Bluebell Line, whose trains are pulled by steam engines rescued from scrapyards, are stranded as the water settles

Sheffield Park

Rains stopped play in this beauty spot, where fine and extensive gardens were laid out by Capability Brown in the 18th century. Tranquil lakes and the sound of an old steam train on the Bluebell Line are also usually there to be enjoyed

There is little evidence of the existence of Sheffield Park's quaint Bluebell Line as a metre of water submerges the area

Arundel

Although this historic town, with its 11th-century castle, escaped the floods, the Wildfowl Park, on 60 acres of meadow land between Swanbourne Lake and the River Arun, was submerged under five feet of water

Cattle find that their customary grazing ground is now under water

Newick
The peace of this old village, whose green comes complete with long-handled pump, was shattered when the River Ouse could no longer be contained

Schoolboys push their bikes through the floodwater on the A272 near Newick

Robertsbridge

It was once a popular resting place for travellers from Hastings to London, but nothing was moving in Robertsbridge when the floods came. This small town was also home to the first Cub Scout pack founded by Baden-Powell

A motorist is stranded in Robertsbridge High Street

Bayham Abbey

The floods added to the damage inflicted in 1537 when Henry VIII dissolved the monasteries and left the abbey in ruins. Bayham, near Royal Tunbridge Wells, lies in the wooded valley of the Teise

The ancient walls of Bayham Abbey are submerged

Lamberhurst

Pavements were upturned and walls collapsed under the strain of water in this village lying on the Kent/Sussex border. Vast vineyards, originated by 16th-century monks, suffered extensive flooding

Main picture: Lamberhurst awash. Right: the scene outside the Chequers pub, which has suffered flooding in the past. Landlady Claire de Garston, centre, has spent £60,000 on repairs and is now thinking of calling it a day

HAYDN WEST, PHOTONEWS

Bodiam

This Kentish village is famed for its moated fairytale castle, which was built in 1390 as a protection against the French. Today, it has a new enemy – water

CHRIS O'DONOGHUE

Bodiam Castle was bequeathed to the National Trust in 1925 and is a favourite tourist spot. But the high waters in the grounds and the swollen River Rother make visiting an impossibility

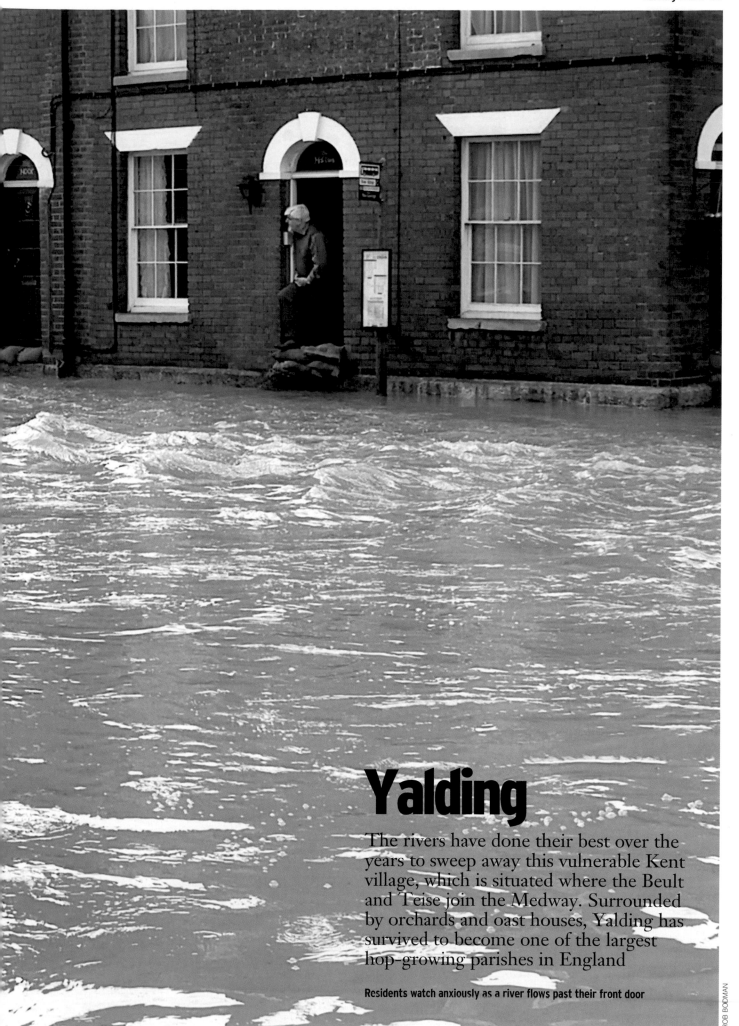

Yalding

The rivers have done their best over the years to sweep away this vulnerable Kent village, which is situated where the Beult and Teise join the Medway. Surrounded by orchards and oast houses, Yalding has survived to become one of the largest hop-growing parishes in England

Residents watch anxiously as a river flows past their front door

ROB BODMAN

Left: flood barriers were no match for the spring tides and torrential rains that caused the River Beult to break its banks, causing the widespread flooding of Yalding.
Above: an Army three-ton lorry lies on its side, deep in water, on the outskirts of the village.
Right: a redundant reminder to campers and riders.
Below: a mother and her children take a canoe ride to safety under the watchful eyes of the fire brigade

Wateringbury

A great storm in 1763 lasted only half an hour but the hailstones lay in heaps for more than a month. The latest natural disaster to hit Wateringbury in the Upper Medway Valley was more prolonged and proved too much for many pleasure craft

A boat comes to rest after swelling waters have washed it away

SCOTT INGLETON, CASSIDY AND LEIGH

South Godstone

Excess water is no stranger to this Surrey village, which includes Lagham Manor, whose name means 'the flooded home'

Traffic comes to a halt and it is time to get out and walk, wade or push on the A22 near South Godstone. There are many springs in the neighbourhood but the volume of water encountered in the floods is almost unprecedented

Etchingham

Rail, road and church were among the many victims in this ancient East Sussex village, lying in the valley of three rivers

Above: the Rev Robert Dixon assesses the damage in the parish church to the 14th-century funeral brasses of the founding family of Etchingham.
Right: parking at the railway station is a high-risk venture.
Left: flooded tracks bring train services to a halt

Tonbridge
A flood barrier was built to protect this historic Kent castle town, but the gates had to be opened when the weight of water became too great

The lock at Tonbridge showing a sluice gate used to stem the flow of the Medway. Today it is wide open. Right: a sign for boat trips, but no takers

Laddingford

A neighbour of Yalding, the riverside location of this Kent village put it at serious risk

Below: a motorist, Tim Richter, from Marden, Kent, rescues belongings from the boot of his stranded car.
Right: two abreast down the road on the edge of Laddingford

PHIL HOUGHTON, KENT NEWS AND PICTURES

MATTHEW FEARN, PA

Maidstone

As flood waters rose, townspeople kept
a day-and-night vigil on Maidstone Bridge.
The bridge survived but eventually the
Medway broke its banks and a vast wave
was sent racing through the centre of town

A canoeist makes his way through church gates
normally used by pedestrians

FLOOD

PART 2 OCTOBER 28-NOVEMBER 15

Even as the waters receded in the South-East, trouble was looming for the whole country. The Atlantic weather system was playing up and forecasters warned of enormous storms heading our way. Saturday, October 28, saw the arrival of the first of a series of storms that were to become so persistent that they seemed like one long, wet and windy nightmare interrupted by a few localised periods of calm.

Day after day the Environment Agency issued new flood warnings apparently covering every river we had ever heard of and many more besides. The catastrophe in the South-East began to pale into relative insignificance as major towns and cities, many of them historic sites originally founded on navigable rivers, succumbed.

In early November Shrewsbury, Worcester and Gloucester fell prey to the raging Severn. Leeds and Manchester were brought to a standstill. The Dales ceased to be havens of rural beauty. Even the M25

New storms caused Britain's already swollen rivers to wreak havoc again

RICHARD AUSTIN, RICHARD AUSTIN NEWS

around London was under waist-high water. The already beleaguered railway system broke down almost entirely, with no trains running south of Manchester. The Taff overflowed at Cardiff. Major rivers in the West Country overspilled and in the city of Exeter thousands of people found themselves without drinking water.

The Army and emergency services drew grateful admiration everywhere. Soldiers were drafted in to fight the Battle of the Ouse to save York and surrounding towns. Even so, the plains of Yorkshire filled with water whose surface area was said to be equivalent to that of Windermere, across the Pennines.

The South-East suffered again and was on permanent alert, with incessant rain and high tides threateninig to make things worse. Estimates of the final cost, though seldom reliable at this stage of a disaster, rose to a heady £2 billion as Britain battled with its oldest adversary, the weather.

A railway engineer has to mind the gap as he inspects a stretch of line which is suspended in mid-air after floods washed away part of the track bed near Exeter. This was just one reason for a series of rail disruptions

RICHARD AUSTIN, RICHARD AUSTIN NEWS

It began with a tornado then back came the rain

Tornadoes are not as rare in Britain as you would think, but they are usually in isolated areas and generally go unreported. The one that hit Bognor Regis in West Sussex on Saturday, October 28, therefore, was meteorologically unexceptional – but exceptionally newsworthy. For days, forecasters had been predicting powerful storms and Britain braced itself for a battering. It got it.

Howling winds and torrential rain laid siege to southern Britain. Coastal regions bore the brunt. At Bognor, caravans were tossed around, trees were uprooted and windows were blown in as winds up to 120mph sucked up debris and scattered it all over the devastated town. Falling trees caused accidents to multiply across the South, killing one man and seriously injuring two in Hindhead, Surrey, and killing a motorcyclist near Taunton in Somerset. On Sunday, the winds were strong enough to overturn an empty Cessna 172 jet at Edinburgh airport.

On Monday, another tornado, this time reaching 150 mph, ripped through Selsey in West Sussex, where bulldozers had been trying to bolster sea defences. It was its second in two years. But the nation had little time to be amazed; it was simply paralysed.

The national rail network, already operating on emergency speed limits after the Hatfield derailment, was at a virtual standstill as 3,000 workers struggled to clear 1,100 trees and branches from the lines. About 70 per cent of the 20,000 miles of railway was out of action: south of Manchester almost no trains ran, while in the North, North-East and Scotland what trains there were moved at a snail's pace.

In London, even the Underground was disrupted when trees fell on overground sections. British Airways cancelled 100 flights from Heathrow, and Dover closed its port, leaving 6,000 passengers aboard ferries tossing about on the stormy seas, some for as long as 20 hours.

In the North, it was not rain that closed roads, but snow. Blizzards blocked the A57 between Manchester and Sheffield and the A66 north of Scotch Corner was blocked by drifts. Six inches of snow fell on the higher parts of Derbyshire and Yorkshire.

There was commuter chaos in Lancashire and Greater Manchester; and 10 per cent of London's workforce failed to make it to work. Elsewhere, motorways became waterways: a section of the M25 orbital motorway around London was waist-high in water. Across the South-East 13,000 homes were without power. In Hastings, East Sussex, a man broke his leg when he was blown 50ft along a road.

The South-West endured more than three inches of rain. More than 100 schools were closed. At Freshford, near Bath, a fire crew had to swim for their lives when their tender was overturned by a torrent. The maze at Longleat in Wiltshire was severely damaged when a 100-year-old oak was blown down. In Exeter, 12,000 properties were *without* water because of burst water mains. The village of Taddiport, north Devon, was under four feet of seething brown water. In Wales, severe flood warnings – "imminent danger to property and life" – were issued for the Cynon and the Taff, which threatened Cardiff. Across Wales, 27 schools were shut.

The next day, water streaming from the heavens and off the Pennines made Hallowe'en a real nightmare for much of Yorkshire. In Leeds, roads resembled canals as the River Aire brimmed over embankments 25ft higher than its normal level.

Dozens of smaller towns closer to the fells were evacuated as the Wharfe, too, overflowed. Bingley arts centre became an emergency shelter. In Keighley, people found refuge in the local swimming baths. Malton in North Yorkshire illustrated how far inland tidal effects were adding to the misery – a seal was spotted 25 miles from the coast. Nearby Norton and Stamford Bridge succumbed to the rising waters of the raging Derwent.

In York, soldiers battled to reinforce defences as the Ouse rose 15ft. Large areas of York were saved by their efforts – but despite them, more than 150 businesses were driven out and the cellars and basements of the Archbishop's Palace were invaded. By Friday November 3, 3,000 people in the city had been forced from their homes.

Bonfire Night was a washout in most areas as the rain resumed, as heavy as ever. Villages around Chichester were swamped as the Lavant burst its banks; the Stour broke clear in Dorset into parts of Bournemouth; Yalding in Kent, recovering from the first onslaught, succumbed once more.

The mighty Severn provided plenty of drama: the ancient centre of Shrewsbury became inaccessible. Downriver in Bewdley in Worcesterhire, swans trod water outside people's homes. In Worcester itself, the water rose to within inches of the arches of its ancient bridge and Gloucester's historic dock fell victim to the watery invader. A new phenomenon – landslides – added to the danger: the landlord of the Britannia Inn in Llangollen, north Wales, narrowly escaped with his life when a slide rammed into his pub.

The Battle of the Ouse continued. York's main defences could hold back the river up to 17ft 10in; by Thursday November 8 the Ouse was within two inches of brimming over into the city. In Barlby, soldiers used Chinook helicopters to distribute 10,000 tons of sandbags to house-holders to keep the Ouse at bay.

Now even the Thames gave way, around Maidenhead and Bray in Berkshire and Walton-on-Thames and Thames Ditton in Surrey, areas thick with the homes of celebrities.

By mid-November the nationwide catastrophe was at its height as the waters rose here and receded there, sometimes returning to already stricken towns and villages. North-South and East-West rail links settled into long-term disruption. A terrible normality was born; even as meteorologists prepared to acknowledge autumn 2000 as the wettest since 1727. Britain was learning to cope with whatever Nature could throw at her.

A child is carried to safety by his father in Sandhurst, Gloucestershire, after rescue teams had prepared a boat to evacuate residents

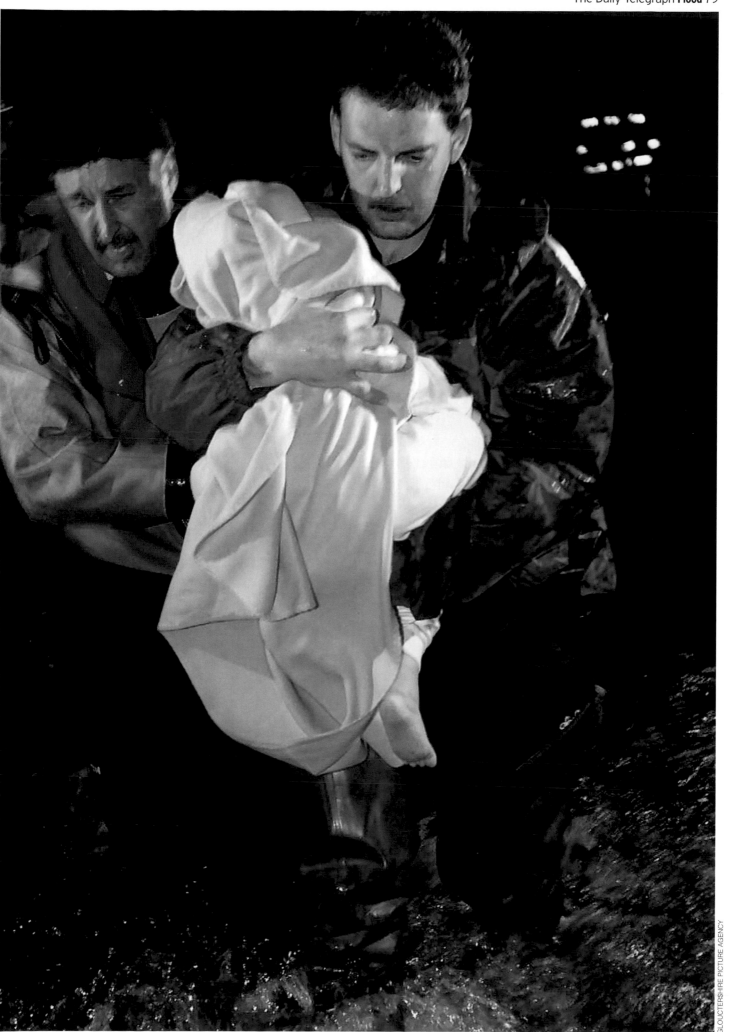

Weather records were broken one after another

Philip Eden
reports on an
unforgettable season
of tornadoes,
98 mph gales,
record depressions
and the curious case
of the self
perpetuating
downpour

Ever since Noah, flooding has been part and parcel of our natural environment, and that is just as true of Britain as it is of many other parts of the world.

It is, I am sure, scant comfort to the inhabitants of Uckfield, Lewes and other towns and villages so badly hit by the mid-October 2000 flood to be told that their disaster was perfectly normal. But it is important to emphasise that there is no need to seek out any "special" reason for the torrential downpours which caused the rivers to rise so dramatically. Rainfall of this intensity, although rare, is by no means unprecedented; in other words, such a rainstorm falls well within the envelope of meteorological fluctuations which characterise the climate of south-east England.

Having said all that, the impact on our homes and communities of the 2000 flood was undoubtedly much higher than a similar flood, say, half a century ago. For this we can blame ourselves: building new estates and roads on flood plains, draining marshes and water meadows, culverting streams and so on. All these things contribute to the severity of flooding along a water course.

The concentration of the mid-October flooding in Sussex and Kent was the result of an exceptional coincidence of meteorological factors. A line of thunderstorms formed along the boundary between two contrasting air-masses stretching approximately from Brighton to Maidstone. This string of storms became aligned along the flow of the southwesterly wind for more than 36 hours so there was no impetus for it to move away. Moreover, the warmth of the English Channel provided sufficient additional energy to the system to cause new storms to generate as the older ones weakened. In effect the downpour was self-perpetuating.

Consequently, the area which received an abnormally large quantity of rain was quite restricted, with four inches or more falling on the tract of countryside extending from Brighton

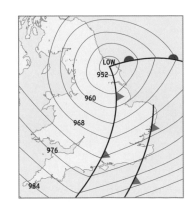

to Crowborough. At Plumpton, near Lewes, 6.85 inches of rain fell in 48 hours – three months' worth in two days.

How does this quantity of rain compare with Britain's biggest ever downpours? The greatest fall ever recorded in the UK was at Martinstown, near Dorchester, when 11 inches of rain fell in 10 hours on July 18, 1955. The famous Hampstead storm of August 15, 1975 produced 6.7 inches – almost the same as Plumpton's two-day total – in just 150 minutes.

This time, as the waters slowly subsided and the October sun at last came out out again, no one could have imagined that worse was to follow. The mid-month deluge in the Garden of England was but a prelude to a nationwide disaster that was to see flood waters lapping around homes and shops and churches from Penzance to Inverness.

After a respite lasting barely two weeks, a series of ferocious Atlantic storms, feeding from the remnants of tropical hurricanes and sustained by the warmth of the ocean waters, swept across the British Isles and neighbouring parts of Europe between October 28 and November 8.

This stormy period began with a tornado which cut a swathe two miles long by 50 yards wide through the Sussex town of Bognor Regis at tea time on Saturday the 28th. Experts estimated the wind speeds in this rapidly rotating vortex may have reached 120 mph. This was the third tornado in three years to create mayhem in this particularly corner of the country – one in Selsey in January 1998 and another at Pagham in September 1999 – but reports of yet another one in Selsey two days later were subsequently discounted. Although there are on average about 40 tornadoes every year in the UK, few of them hit urban areas, so most go unreported by the national news media.

The severe gale which battered England and Wales during the early hours of October 30 ranked alongside

A record Low: The depression of October 30 (left) was a record-breaker. The barometric pressure at its centre sank to 950 millibars, the lowest ever recorded in England in October

The floods return to rivers across the country

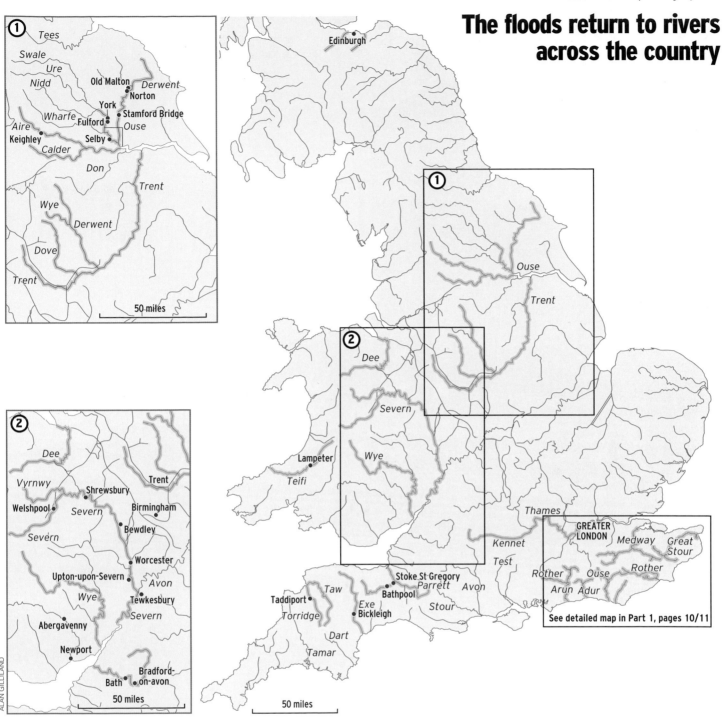

the worst during the past 10 years. The depression responsible was itself a record-breaker. As it travelled across north Wales and northern England the barometric pressure at the centre of the "low" sank to 950 millibars (28.05 inches of mercury), the lowest ever recorded in England in October, surpassing even Michael Fish's "hurricane" of 1987. Household barometers pointed resolutely at "Very Stormy". At the height of the gale, the wind blew at a sustained speed of 50 to 60mph with peak gusts of 80 to 90mph. At Mumbles, near Swansea, and the Needles, at the western extremity of the Isle of Wight, gusts of 98mph were recorded. Although insurance

companies were predicting a surprisingly small level of claims for gale damage, road and rail travel was completely disrupted in many parts of England and Wales as surface water conspired with uprooted trees to block major transport arteries. The fact that most of them were still in leaf contributed to the large number of trees brought down.

The floods which followed were caused by repeated nationwide downpours rather than by the localised cloudbursts which created the earlier flood in South East England. An average of five to six inches of rain fell in 10 days over England and Wales.

Flooding on short rivers, such as

those of south Wales and the West Country, came and went within 36 hours of each downpour, but the nation's longer rivers, such as the Yorkshire Ouse and the Severn, suffered a gradual build-up of water levels followed by a prolonged peak and then a slow but steady decline. It takes about five days for the crest of a flood to travel from the slopes of the Pennines and the North York Moors into the Ouse and then out into the tidal waters of the Humber.

The experts are now warning of further floods during the winter of 2000-2001. The land is waterlogged, the rivers are in spate and any future spell of disturbed "Atlantic" weather could have dire consequences.

1947 vs 2000: This year's floods were Britain's worst *inland* floods since 1947 The peak water levels then were no higher than this year's but the floods affected 1,000 square miles compared with an estimated 300-400 square miles this time

On a clear day the seaside town of Selsey, at the tip of the Selsey Bill peninsula in West Sussex, boasts splendid views of the Isle of Wight. But as storm-force winds

e a violent assault it is hard to see a hand in front of your face. More than 1,000 buildings were damaged when a tornado hit the town in 1998

MICK YOUNG, M&Y PORTSMOUTH

MICHAEL STEPHENS,PA

RICHARD AUSTIN, RICHARD AUSTIN NEWS

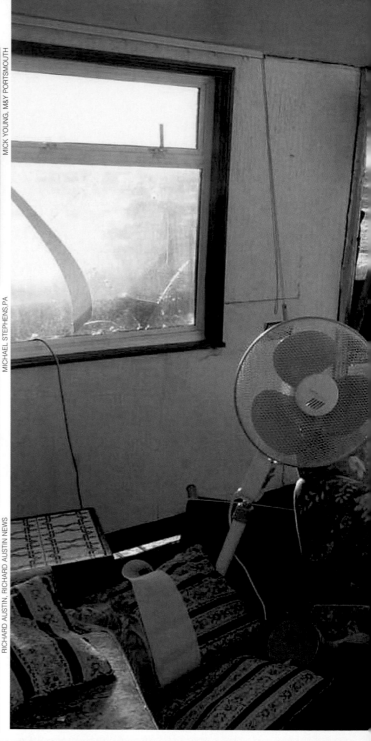

GERRY PENNY, EPA

Clockwise from top left:
Wreckage left by the storm which struck Riverside Caravan Park at South Bersted, near Bognor Regis, in West Sussex.
The sea view from the interior of a chalet after a tornado hit West Sand Caravan Park, Selsey.
Flying debris ruins homes on Hayling Island, Hampshire.
High seas crash over the harbour wall at Newhaven, East Sussex, disrupting ferry services to France.
The resort of Lyme Regis, Dorset, faces a pounding from huge waves.
At Dover storm-watchers risk being engulfed by remaining too close to the promenade

An almost welcome change from floods and storms as snow and slush make the going tough in the village of Farsley in Leeds

Ploughing through the snow on the A683 in Cumbria. Right: Debbie and Robert Gordon next to their two crushed cars in Beckenham, Kent

A car is flattened by a collapsed roof in Robertsbridge, East Sussex, after floods and high winds. Right: Wind destroys a tree in Brighton

A 100-year-old oak tree falls on the world's longest hedge maze, at Longleat, Wiltshire. Right: clearing the Tube rails in West London

Rail travel is hazardous in some places as trains run the risk of being hit by trees. These incidents are at West Bromwich and Hounslow

Wind and torrential rain are responsible for the demise of this Peugeot, which suffers damage from a tree trunk in Hornchurch, Essex

Tourist attractions and historic landmarks alike were victims of flood waters as the city of York succumbed to flooding after days of desperate resistance

KINGS ARMS

York

The much-loved city, a magnet for tourists, became the focus of national attention as thousands of people were evacuated from their homes.

Eventually, after anxious days and nights for the population, the multi-million pound flood defences capitulated to the River Ouse, swollen to a torrent by waters off the Pennines

DAN CHUNG, REUTERS

Clockwise from top left: An emergency vehicle ploughs through the flood water as the River Ouse rises 15 feet above its normal level.
The Archbishop of York, Dr David Hope, outside Bishopthorpe Palace, his official residence, where the cellars and basement, containing ancient papers and artefacts, were flooded.
The submerged grounds of Bishopthorpe Palace.
Tea time for a Royal Signals driver, courtesy of a York resident, Mrs Sharon Grant: more than 250 soldiers were on standby during the emergency in the area.

Another resident, Malcolm Goodwin, takes to the streets armed with umbrella and waders.
For one woman a good old-fashioned firemen's lift was the only means of rescue.
York's town cryer, John Redpath, fulfils his duties in a manner of which his predecessors would have been proud

JOHN GILES, PA

JOHN GILES, PA

CHRIS BARKER, PA

A lone canoeist enjoys a day
at the races at York after the
River Ouse had reached its
highest level for 400 years

Clockwise from top left:
Soldiers add sandbags to the existing flood barrier at York.
Marooned but safe; two floors up is one of the best places to be.
The Prime Minister, Tony Blair, pays a visit to the stricken city.
Sgt Mike Stubbs, of North Yorkshire Police, assumes a new role to deliver the daily pint.
For the time being, the river warning sign is superfluous.
As yet another deluge is forecast, firemen top up the flood defences, with York Minster in the background

Norton

Villagers' problems by the bucketful

Janet Fearnley tries to keep out water from the Derwent but finds it a futile struggle. Norton, in North Yorkshire, famous as a centre for training racehorses, has previous experience of flooding. The river last burst its banks in 1999

Selby

Residents are asked to go back to school as their homes are no longer safe

People in the market town of Selby, who had to be evacuated, find refuge at Brayton High School.
Selby's position, on the River Ouse between York and the River Humber, makes it a high-risk area as the rivers fill up throughout Yorkshire

Stamford Bridge

The Battle of Stamford Bridge is fought once more; only this time flood water is the opponent

Rescuers get the green light, or go it alone

Fulford

The overflowing River Ouse expands its territory to engulf vast areas around York

Postman Keith Jameson gets a lift on a council lorry in Fulford

Old Malton

There are three neighbouring Maltons in North Yorkshire: Roman, Old and New. But Nature did not discriminate when the storms arrived in this historic centre of Rydale. Like Norton, the area was hit by floods in March, 1999

CRAIG STENNETT

Main picture: a deceptive peace descends on Old Malton after the flood water has settled.
Far left: Juliet Stimson, landlady of the Royal Oak, decides to stay open whatever the weather.
Left: an aerial view of the flooded town centre of Malton

ROSS-PARRY AGENCY

LORNE CAMPBELL, GUZELIAN

Keighley

With the woollen industry
a thing of the past,
Keighley is said to keep its
head above water as the
centre for shoppers in
middle Airedale. It just
about kept its reputation
intact, although 200 homes
had to be evacuated as the
Aire flooded

Clockwise from top left:
A fireman carries a toddler away from danger in Keighley.
Flood evacuees from the Stockbridge area of Keighley take refuge in the local leisure centre.
Wheelie bins tumble through the streets of Stockbridge, becoming trapped under a car bumper.
With the fear of more flooding imminent, residents don't know what is around the corner

Shrewsbury

The medieval streets of
Shropshire's county town
include the aptly-named
Fish Street. But few
ventured out of the black
and white buildings when
the Severn, which enfolds
the town in a great loop,
spilled over

Clockwise from top left:
There looks to be no dry escape for these
cyclists in Shrewsbury town centre.
The aerial view shows how the town was cut off
after the Severn overflowed.
A young resident gets caught out when
water-depth exceeds wellington-boot depth.
A close call for a youngster who tries to avoid a
soaking amid the period street furniture

JASON CAIRNDUFF, NEWS TEAM INTERNATIONAL

Bewdley

In the Middle Ages, Bewdley, in Worcestershire, was built on a hillside above the River Severn. It is only since the development of the riverside that property has become vulnerable to flooding

Clockwise from top left: For sale, with river view; Stan Lewis feeds the swans with

DAVID BURGES

...ng to leave his shop; a policeman on the bench; water devastates a fish bar; residents become housebound as the flood water laps against their homes

Worcester

Few were unaffected when the floods hit Worcester. The Army helped move hospital patients and the cricket ground was submerged

Above: a more than wet wicket at Worcestershire County Cricket Club. Right: clouds hang threateningly over the Severn. Below: water nearly engulfs the old town br

Upton-on-Severn

It was once protection against invaders, but overnight the river became a foe

Boats appear a pleasant option at Upton-on-Severn, Worcestershire

Tewkesbury

Situated at the junction of the Severn and the Avon, Tewkesbury soon became a casualty

**Far right: an aerial view of the route of the M50 in Gloucestershire.
Right: only roads on higher ground in the town remain passable**

Llandrinio

When Tony and Liz Dawson's farm near Llandrinio, Powys, was inundated, the couple's first concern was for the welfare of their animals. So it was open house

Liz Dawson takes a back seat at
Lower House Farm, Llandrinio,
as it becomes a temporary home
to a flock of sheep which
needs shelter from the storm
(see also next page)

Liz and Tony Dawson's home in Llandrinio on the Welsh borders becomes an indoor farmyard as they decide to share it with their calves as well as sheep

Ruthin

A market town pays
the price for being
down by the riverside

Guests have to be determined to
reach this hotel in Mwrog Street in
Ruthin, which lies at the end of the
Vale of Clwyd

Welshpool

Flights are grounded
as the airport vanishes
under water

Below: appearances can be deceptive.
These onlookers are standing beside
Welshpool airport, Powys

Newport

Newport relies on river and sea to provide the town with jobs. But the floods put its relationship with water to the test

Drivers take their time as they make their way through Newport, Gwent. The road is only just navigable

MARK LEWIS, REUTERS

DRAGON NEWS AND PICTURES

Lampeter

Low-lying land is no place to lead a horse to water

A wild horse forages near Lampeter, Ceredigion, but many animals were forced on to high ground

Abergavenny

A landslide leaves a barrier of mud to block the Gateway to Wales

Nestling in the Usk Valley, Abergavenny is the traditional Gateway to Wales and to the Brecon Beacons National Park.
Right: the floods caused a landslide which blocked the A465 Heads of the Valleys road near the town

HUW EVANS

Bradford-on-Avon

Watery tales of a riverbank in a corner of Wiltshire that grew up around a 'broad ford' across the Avon

Left: from where young Harvey Walton stands, the floods in the Cotswold-stone town of Bradford-on-Avon are fun.
Top right: the town centre is not a popular place for pedestrians.
Right: Anthony Forsyth boards his coracle to find a drier way of travelling

Bath

When the River Avon turned the splendour of Bath into a washout

Far right: the home of Bath Rugby Football Club under flood water from the River Avon.
Centre: in Bathford, near Bath, a policeman comes to the aid of a stranded youngster.
Right: an Avon and Somerset fire tender is put out of action in Freshford, Bath

Stoke St Gregory

Eels take the trouble to swim 4,000 miles from the Sargasso Sea to enjoy Somerset's River Parrett. It runs by Stoke St Gregory, parts of which are dangerously susceptible to flooding. But one resident has taken matters into his own hands

Above and left: retired naval officer Douglas Billington rows past his home in Stoke St Gregory, near Taunton, in the days when it was the most flooded house in Somerset.
Right: now Mr Billington has built his own flood defences out of clay, and his home has fared well in the floods of 2000

Bathpool

Standing on the Taunton to Bridgwater canal, this Somerset village in cider country found its attractions as a popular campsite diminished by the downpour

Far right: Leslie Keitch struggles to get home as floods fill the streets of Bathpool.
Right: cars still have somewhere to park, even though they have nowhere to go

Taddiport

Built on the River Torridge, this Devon
farming village feared for its livestock

Top: the Toll House is transformed into an island.
Right: flood waters spread over several acres of Taddiport.
Below: beef cattle are trapped at Thorverton, near Exeter

Bickleigh

Still raging after all these years, the river that inspired Paul Simon to write Bridge Over Troubled Water

Right: Paul Simon wrote one of his finest songs after seeing this stretch of the River Exe at Bickleigh.
Left: a flock of sheep is saved from flooded fields in Colyford, near Exeter

RICHARD AUSTIN, RICHARD AUSTIN NEWS

London

Many who work in the capital were forced to stay at home as public transport was severely disrupted

TONY LIPSCOMBE, PA

ANDY GATT, PIXEL

Clockwise from top left: A shopper wades through the waters of Knightsbridge. A stalled car brings traffic to a halt in East London. The miserable scene at night on the roads of Waltham Abbey, Essex. The driver of the Number 2 bus to Marylebone Station, pictured at Crystal Palace, does his best to keep going

RUSSELL BOYCE, REUTERS

ROB WHELHAM, MCLELLAN

A resident of London Colney, St Albans, Hertfordshire, floats to safety, courtesy of the fire brigade after the River Colne had flooded the area

South-East

Rivers overflowing and homes swamped; communities throughout the region were fearful of what the heavens might bring down on them next. Some had realised that their properties might be at risk, but they had not expected such a relentless onslaught of water

Guests climb aboard at the Reading Moat House Hotel. Right: 'Alice' goes swimming in Guildford. The statue honours a former resident, Lewis Carroll

The flat land of Reading, Berkshire, is saturated as water spreads over many acres of fields. The River Kennet also rose several feet in the town centre

The River Loddon is immortalised in the poetry of Alexander Pope. Here, it overflows as it runs through Sherfield on Loddon, Hampshire

Above: snakes which inhabit the banks of the River Medway in Kent are shy types, preferring to conceal themselves among the reeds. But the floods forced them out to seek calmer waters.
Right: safety first for four children in Yalding, Kent, as they make their way to school holding hands

Kent and East Sussex hit again

Villagers and townspeople throughout Kent and East Sussex had little time to recover from the unpleasant and expensive experience of having their homes invaded by torrents of filthy water. Word soon went out that they were in for more of the same. In some places, the floods were worse second time around because they were now accompanied by fierce winds

Top: no doggy paddling in the village of Yalding today.
Middle: two young women are saddled up for a spot of shopping in Yalding. Here, they collect their change from a village shopkeeper.
Right: the parish church in Etchingham, East Sussex, falls victim to a second bout of flooding

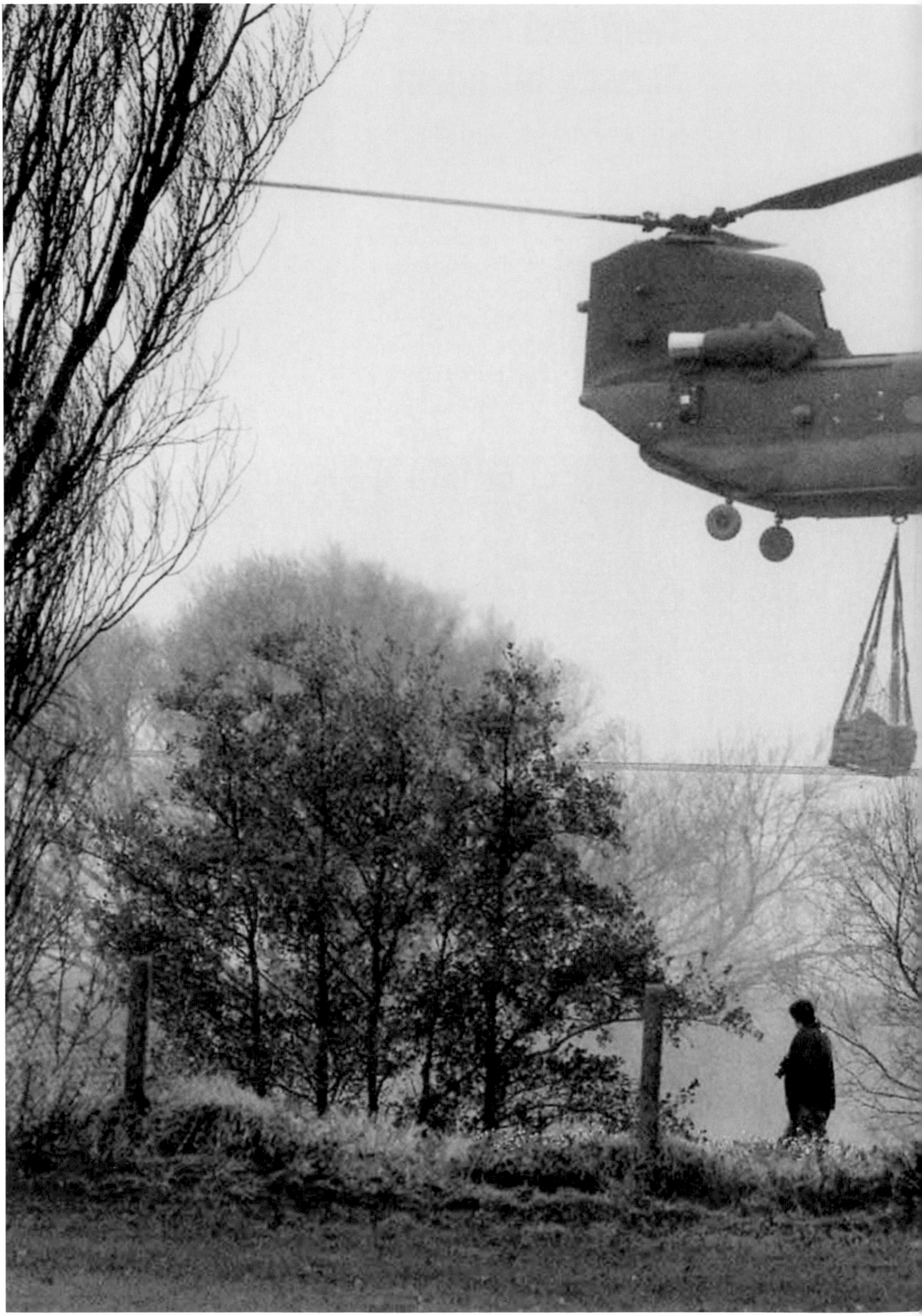

An Army Chinook helicopter drops
sandbags to prevent the
floods spreading in the village of
Barlby, North Yorkshire

FLOOD
The Daily Telegraph

CASSIDY & LEIGH

Creative Director Clive Crook
Editorial Projects Director George Darby
Publisher Susannah Charlton
Pictures Bob Bodman
Designer Simon Khalil
Graphics Alan Gilliland
Production/text Harry Coen, Bill Owen
Research Jackie Holland
Special contributors W.F.Deedes, Philip Eden

Repro Colour Department, Telegraph Group Ltd

Maps depicting predicted maximum flooding extent (pages 10-11): data supplied by kind permission of the Environment Agency © Institute of Hydrology, MAFF and Ordnance Survey

Technical note

The use of digital cameras for the rapid transmission of images for newspaper use means that images in this volume, particularly those used at large size, may in some instances lack the very sharp definition normally achieved in high quality book printing.

First published 2000 by Telegraph Books, an imprint of the Telegraph Group Ltd, 1 Canada Square, Canary Wharf, London E14 5DT in association with Froglets Publications Ltd, Brasted, Chart, Westerham, Kent,TN16 1LY. Telephone 01959 562 972

ISBN 0 86367 998 6

Printed and bound by Giunti Industrie Grafiche, Iolo Prato, Italy.